Lucky Cat

Thank you to Hisayuki Ishimatsu, Head of the Japanese Collection
and Reference Services of the University of California at Berkeley's
East Asian Library, for help with translation and research.

ISBN-10: 0-8118-4121-9
ISBN-13: 978-0-8118-4121-4
Design by Amy Ennis
Photographs by Marc Herman, except pp. 5, 38, and cover by Steve Mockus
Manufactured in China

10

Chronicle Books LLC
680 Second Street
San Francisco, California 94107
www.chroniclebooks.com

Lucky Cat

まねき猫

He Brings You Good Luck

Laurel Wellman

CHRONICLE BOOKS

SAN FRANCISCO

まねき猫

4

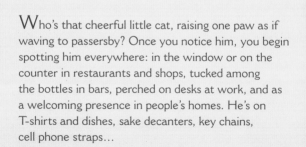

Who's that cheerful little cat, raising one paw as if waving to passersby? Once you notice him, you begin spotting him everywhere: in the window or on the counter in restaurants and shops, tucked among the bottles in bars, perched on desks at work, and as a welcoming presence in people's homes. He's on T-shirts and dishes, sake decanters, key chains, cell phone straps…

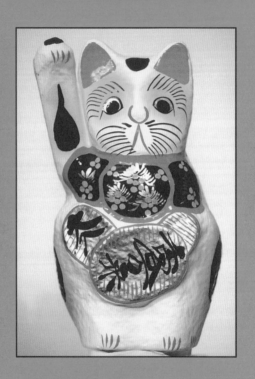

The little cat is Maneki Neko—which means Beckoning Cat, though he's often just called Lucky Cat—symbol of prosperity, fortune in business, and general good luck. He's been around for almost 150 years, though some popular legends claim he's much older. Still, in that century and a half, his popularity has carried Lucky Cat from his origins in Japan to Hong Kong, China, Singapore, Thailand, and around the world to become a pop culture celebrity all his own.

Maneki Neko figurines appear in a dazzling variety of styles, all with their own charm and significance. Special meanings created by details such as which paw a Lucky Cat is raising, what color he's painted, and even what he's carrying, mean there's a Lucky Cat for every taste—and for everyone. Some Maneki Nekos beckon love, others attract wealth or success in studies. Lucky Cats may be crafted of papier-mâché, cast in porcelain or plastic, or carved from stone or wood; they may be simple and unadorned, or ornately glazed and painted. They may be roly-poly or sleek and elegant. Even their facial expressions vary—

ranging from serene to somber, from cheerful to meditative, from enigmatic to blissful.

For all this diversity, however, Maneki Neko is a unique icon. Though his image has been used to sell everything from beer to electronics, and his history is a little racy, the Beckoning Cat has transcended his origins and come to embody good wishes, hope, happiness, and luck itself. Whether you place your own Lucky Cat in your home, at work, or elsewhere, you can always count on his cheerful support. As the Maneki Neko Club, a Japan-based international society dedicated to promoting the Lucky Cat, says, "Fill the world with Maneki Neko!"

Legends

We know that Maneki Neko's origins are in Japan and date to the Edo period (1603–1868). But as is often the case with mysterious and wonderful things, a number of competing legends purport to explain his history. For example, at least two temples would like to claim Lucky Cat as their own, and their tales of the

"original" Beckoning Cat naturally contradict each other.

One of these is the Lucky Cat legend familiar to some Westerners—the story of a samurai, Lord Naotaka Ii, an actual historical figure who lived at the beginning of the Edo period. As the story goes, the lord and his entourage were returning from battle to their home district of Hikone, near present-day Tokyo. (In some versions of the tale, the lord is simply a wealthy man out hunting.) As it began to rain, the group came upon a small, run-down temple in the woods inhabited by a monk—who, though nearly destitute, kept a little white cat named Tama. As Naotaka took shelter under a tree near the temple, he noticed Tama sitting in the temple's gateway. To his surprise, the cat raised her paw and seemed to beckon him inside. Enchanted, the lord dismounted from his horse and entered the temple grounds, whereupon a bolt of lightning struck the tree under which he had just been standing. Tama had saved his life.

In gratitude, Naotaka proclaimed that the temple would henceforth be his family temple. From that

point on, the Gotoku-ji temple enjoyed the patronage of the feudal lord, as well as a considerable rise in fortune. When Tama finally died, she was buried on the temple grounds and the first Maneki Neko statue was created to commemorate her.

Whether or not there actually was a Tama, there is a Gotoku-ji temple, in what is now the western Tokyo suburb of Setagaya, and hundreds of cats are buried on its grounds. People who wish to petition for the well-being of their cats, or for other personal causes, come to the temple with *ema* (prayer boards). It is also possible to buy a Maneki Neko statue there, and the grounds feature wooden shelves lined with them as offerings. And perhaps because some versions of the story make the additional claim that Tama was in fact Kannon (the Japanese name for Kuan Yin, the popular Goddess of Compassion) in cat form, the Gotoku-ji temple contains a statue of Shofoku Kanzeon (Fortune-Beckoning Kannon) within its cat shrine.

The second temple-based Lucky Cat legend centers on the Shonenji temple in Kyoto, which is popularly known as the Nekodera, or Cat Temple. Again, a poor monk kept a cat; one day, feeling discouraged, he asked the animal why it never did anything to help him. The cat disappeared, and the next day the monk was surprised by a visit from two representatives of a wealthy nearby family, who told him the lord's daughter had died in the night and had asked, just before her death, to be buried at the temple. Apparently, the cat had entered her soul and inspired her to make the request. From then on, the temple, and the monk, enjoyed the patronage of the family. The Shonenji temple now contains a popular pet cemetery.

A different and more macabre Maneki Neko legend, purportedly dating to about 1800, is recounted in

Amaury Saint-Gilles's *Mingei: Japan's Enduring Folk Arts*. In this account, two rival teahouses outside the gate of the Eko-in temple in Ryogoku, Tokyo, each placed a porcelain cat statue—one painted gold, the other silver—outside its front door in an attempt to attract business. Nevertheless, the owner of the Golden Cat Teahouse still found herself short of cash, and she convinced a merchant patron to lend her a large sum of money. Unfortunately, the money wasn't really his to lend—it belonged to a friend, and when his friend asked for the money back, the merchant was unable to repay. He resolved to express his remorse by committing suicide. Just as he was about to throw himself off a nearby bridge, the teahouse owner happened to pass by, and when he explained the situation, she decided to join him in a double suicide. The resulting notoriety ensured the financial success of the Golden Cat Teahouse, and the public became convinced, despite the body count, that this was proof of the fortune-beckoning talents of the porcelain cat statue. Sensing a business opportunity, local manufacturers

began selling copies of the statue, and Maneki Neko was born.

In a less dramatic variation on this tale, the two cats stood outside rival ramen shops in Asakusa. At first, only one of the shops had a cat, and all the customers went to it until the other shop got a cat of its own. The power of the Lucky Cat was demonstrated by his ability to balance the equation.

Perhaps the original model for Maneki Neko was the pet cat of a nineteenth-century money changer, one of whose regular clients was a fishmonger. The fishmonger liked the money changer's cat and always brought it a piece of fish when he visited. Unfortunately, the fishmonger got sick and eventually became so ill he couldn't work. One day, on the brink of starvation, he opened his door and found two gold *koban* (coins) outside.

With the money he was able to afford a doctor, and eventually he recovered. But when he returned after his long absence to see the money changer, the cat wasn't there. Asking after his little friend, the fish-monger was told that after the apparent theft of two gold *koban*, the only suspect, the cat, had been put to death as a thief. Sobbing, the fishmonger told his story. All were overcome with grief, and to commemorate the good-hearted cat, they crafted the first Maneki Neko statue.

The Beckoning Cat's true historic association with the culture of the Pleasure Quarters (red-light districts) of Edo and other towns is expressed in still another, somewhat more gruesome Maneki Neko legend. In this story, set in the mid-Edo period, a courtesan named Usugumo owned a pet cat she loved very much and which, in return, was extremely loyal to her.

One evening, she and the cat were walking through the garden of the geisha house to the bathhouse; suddenly, at the doorway to the bathhouse, the cat leapt in front of her and blocked her path, hissing and raising his paw to claw at her robes if she dared step forward. (In another version, Usugumo is taking a bath, and the cat keeps trying to climb into the water.) She screamed for help. Bystanders took this apparent attack as evidence that the cat had become possessed by evil spirits, and the owner of the geisha house (or someone else who just happened to have a sword handy) lopped off the animal's head.

Magically, the cat's head flew up into the rafters of the bathhouse to bite and kill a poisonous snake that had been lurking there, ready to strike Usugumo. The loyal cat, by refusing to let her enter the building, had been doing all it could to save her life. To try to ease Usugumo's grief, a customer gave her a wooden statuette of a cat; this, too, is supposed to be the original Maneki Neko.

A final Lucky Cat legend tells the story of an old woman who kept a beloved pet cat until she grew so poor she was nearly forced to give it up. The cat, however, appeared to her in a dream and told her to model a clay image of it. She did so, and it sold. The old woman made more cat statuettes, and they continued to sell. This saved her—and the clever cat—from destitution, and began the tradition of making (and, more important, selling) Maneki Nekos.

History

Maneki Neko is a popular folk symbol with plenty of mythology behind it, but almost no historical record exists of the true origins of Lucky Cat—probably because the cat statuettes were never considered high art and were therefore overlooked by historians.

Maneki Neko's business-drawing reputation may come from the superstition that if a cat washes its face, a guest will arrive. This superstition has a couple

of possible foundations in fact. The first is that if a cat feels nervous or uncertain, it often will groom itself—so a cat who sees strangers approaching may wash its face. And since cats spend a significant portion of their waking hours absorbed in fussing over their fur, it's a safe bet that at some point a visitor will appear soon after a cat has been grooming itself.

It's also possible that the way in which cats wash themselves inspired the superstition. Anyone who's seen a cat washing its face knows the cat will wet its paw and rub it against the sides of its face. This motion could, with a little imagination, be interpreted as the palm-down beckoning gesture customary in Asia.

It is difficult to say precisely when Lucky Cat figurines became fashionable. Several museum exhibition catalogs date examples of the statues as early as the eighteenth century. A different "lucky cat" figurine—Marujimeneko, a mother cat who carried a kitten on her back—enjoyed a swell of popularity in the nineteenth century, but never achieved the pervasive and enduring status of the Lucky Cat himself.

The best estimate is that Maneki Neko first began to appear widely during the late Edo period, sometime in the mid-nineteenth century. It was at this time that the cat was used as a lucky talisman to beckon customers to brothels (just as the prostitutes often advertised themselves by sitting in the brothels' screened front porches, calling and beckoning to potential clients). Reinforcing this connection is the mid-nineteenth-century slang term for prostitute: *neko* (cat). Some carved wooden signs, or *kanban*, advertising brothels of that era even depicted a beckoning cat. (These are early examples of what was to become an entire *maneki kanban* [beckoning sign] genre, whose other popular symbols included a beckoning Tanuki [the "raccoon dog" of folklore], or Okame, the Goddess of Mirth.)

The Pleasure Quarters of the Edo Period were glamorous centers of art and entertainment, and life within them was not seen as shameful or disreputable. In fact, top courtesans, or *tayu*, were icons of beauty and femininity the way movie stars are today; they

lived lives of wealth and celebrity, surrounded by servants and luxury. People even collected their portraits, which were often created by well-known artists such as Hiroshige.

A major reason the Beckoning Cat's popularity spread beyond the Pleasure Quarters was probably a late-nineteenth-century ban by the Japanese government on the rural folk tradition of phallic worship, in which farmers honored replica phalluses in rituals meant to ensure good crops. This was also a tradition in many brothels, where a shelf called an *engi-dana* near the entrance displayed lucky talismans (including wooden, bamboo, papier-mâché, or clay phallic images) to which the brothel owner and prostitutes prayed in hopes of good business that day.

This custom was not especially popular with authorities during the samurai-dominated Edo period—some commentators of the time decried such "low" traditions and would have liked to see them replaced with the more refined mores and customs of *bushido*, or samurai-class culture—but it

was tolerated. By the time the Meiji government took power in 1868, however, Japan's contact with Western nations had increased dramatically, and this tolerance was at an end. American commodore Matthew Perry, who landed in Japan in 1854, had persuaded the country's government to end its 250 years of isolationism, in part by demonstrating the implied threat of the United States' superior military. Japan was forced to sign an unequal trade treaty with the United States, and it later signed similarly unfavorable treaties with Great Britain, Russia, France, and the Netherlands. The influx of foreign currency destabilized Japan and contributed to the fall of the shogunate.

In the aftermath of these events, the new Meiji regime was intent on restoring Japan to glory, which it saw required transforming the country from an isolated, feudal, agrarian society into a global military and economic power. The government was thus very concerned with presenting Japan as a modernized country, and the idea that Westerners might happen upon remnants of primitive phallic worship was a factor in the government's 1872 ban on the manufacture, sale, or display of the phallus statuettes.

This seems to have provided exactly the sort of lucky break the Lucky Cat needed. Maneki Neko became the preferred legal substitute for the phallic images. (Though scholar Shoichi Inoue makes note of a Maneki Neko statuette created with a secret compartment in which the offending phallus could be hidden.) Soon Maneki Neko's appeal was too great to be contained within the confines of one industry— or even one country. Lucky Cat began to appear in bars, restaurants, and then homes, and by the turn of the twentieth century was being mass-produced in many areas of Japan. But that was only the beginning. Today, Lucky Cat figurines are made across Asia and sold around the world.

The Basic Cat

It may seem obvious that the beckoning gesture defines a Beckoning Cat, but it is specifically through the welcoming gesture of much of Asia—palm facing down—that the Lucky Cat brings good fortune. To many Westerners, the Maneki Neko statues they see in restaurants and other businesses appear to be waving—even waving goodbye. Some less traditional Lucky Cats, manufactured for the Western market, make the palm-up beckoning gesture; these statuettes, sometimes called "Dollar Cats," may also feature blue eyes and hold a coin painted with a dollar sign, rather than the traditional Japanese *koban*.

There is great significance attached to the issue of which paw—left or right—is doing the beckoning, and some controversy about which is "better." It's generally believed that the right paw beckons fortune (specifically, financial prosperity), while the left paw beckons guests or customers. But there are deeper layers of folk meaning: The right paw is sometimes said to beckon

men, the left paw, women. There are also regional quirks and distinctions; in Kyoto, for instance, business owners may choose to display a Maneki Neko with its right paw raised, while owners of bars and restaurants prefer a statuette that beckons with its left paw.

According to the Maneki Neko Club, older, more traditional Lucky Cats beckon with their left paws. In fact, some people decry the increasing popularity of the right-paw Beckoning Cat as a sign of the materialism afflicting global culture, though perhaps that is rather too harsh an assessment to fall on the cat's little shoulders. Still, it's possible to cover all the bases and find a Maneki Neko that beckons with both paws simultaneously, or a set of two cats, each beckoning with a different paw. There are also cat statuettes that hold their palms earnestly together in front of them, not beckoning so much as supplicating.

Whichever paw is raised, it traditionally rises to just above whisker level. On the theory that a longer arm might give the cat an advantage in snatching passing fortune, cats with extra-long arms sometimes

stretching well above their heads—have become popular, especially among Japanese Lucky Cat fans weary of the country's economic stagnation. Unluckily, though, these longer arms may break more easily.

The classic Maneki Neko wears a bell around its neck. This convention recalls a time when cats were rare and expensive in Japan. (It is thought cats were imported to Japan from China to protect Buddhist texts from rats and mice, just as they are believed to have been imported from India to China.) Because the animals were so valuable, they were often kept tied up, and the bell, which could be used to locate the cat if it managed to get loose, was a backup security feature. Maneki Neko's bell is suspended from a collar, which is usually red—a color associated with good fortune.

Beneath the bell, many Lucky Cat figurines— perhaps half—sport some sort of neckwear. The most common is a bib, or *yodarekake* (literally, "saliva catcher"). The next most popular is a *noren*-style neckpiece, so called because it is formed of flaps

of fabric much like the familiar half-curtains in Japanese restaurant doorways. A scarf or bandana is a less popular fashion look. Common colors for any of these neckpieces are red, green, and blue, sometimes with decorative gold accents.

Though it's a given that Maneki Neko is more fashion-forward than most felines, historical illustrations don't seem to indicate that bibs or scarves were popular for pet cats in Edo- or Meiji-period Japan, and anyone who lives with a cat knows why: Most cats hate wearing anything around their necks. One possible explanation for Lucky Cat's neckwear, suggested by holdings in the Tokyo Edo Museum, is that it may be a design element left over from an earlier fad seen in dog statuettes. These bib-wearing statuettes were placed in pregnant women's bedrooms to ensure easy childbirth and a healthy baby, and to keep evil spirits away; the bibs likely emphasized their connection with babies. Another possible explanation is that the scarf recalls the accessory traditionally seen in depictions of Jizo, the Japanese name for a popular Buddhist

bodhisattva who appears as a child-monk and—according to Zen priest, author, and Jizo expert Chozen Roshi—is supposed to protect babies and children, the poor, and the sick.

Maneki Neko's tail is often quite short, though as with other aspects of the Lucky Cat, there is wide variety. Traditional Maneki Neko figurines are modeled after Japanese bobtails—a breed of cat that has existed in Japan for centuries—whose truncated tail should be, according to the show standards of the international Cat Fanciers Association, no more than three inches long.

Finally, Maneki Neko is usually seen holding a gold *koban*, an oval-shaped Japanese coin dating to the Tokugawa shogunate, which was in power throughout the Edo period. The real *koban* was a one-*ryou* coin, a basic unit of currency. The *koban* held by Maneki Neko is traditionally depicted as being worth one million *ryou*. However, many Lucky Cats don't carry a *koban*; some merely beckon fortune rather than bringing it with them, and others carry fish, kittens, or whole sacks of money.

Beyond the Basic Cat

Maneki Neko is always a beckoning cat, but this basic requirement places little restriction on designers' imaginations. Indeed, one of the delights of Maneki Neko is its infinite variety. According to the Maneki Neko Club, which has conducted exhaustive research, the prevalent style among older Maneki Nekos is the Fushimi style, which likely dates to the 1870s. Fushimi-style cats have relatively small eyes; there is no "eyeliner" emphasizing them, and their pupils are small black dots. Most were made of earthenware, and production was small scale.

The Mikawa-style cat is thought to have become popular around 1925. It features a slightly larger pupil and a thin line emphasizing the eye. This style of cat could be earthenware, but some were porcelain, and the cats became slightly larger.

In the post–World War II era, the Tsunesuberi style of cat—the one most frequently seen today— appeared on the scene. With a large head, large eyes, large pupils, and a thick application of eyeliner, its face

has a distinctive, stylized appearance, unlike the more naturalistic earlier Lucky Cat designs. These inexpensive Maneki Neko figurines, common in sushi restaurants and Asian neighborhoods in Western cities, are not the focus of the most serious Lucky Cat aficionados, although there are collectors who own hundreds or even thousands of Tsunesuberi-style Lucky Cats.

    High-end Maneki Neko figurines are made by some of Japan's leading porcelain producers, such as Seto-yaki, Imari-yaki, and Kutani-yaki. Porcelain Seto and Imari cats are often pure white and of a naturalistic design; unlike Tsunesuberi cats, their heads are in proportion to their bodies. Imari and Seto cats may also feature stylized red and black "tortoise" spots. Kutani cats are of naturalistic proportions but may showcase the manufacturer's porcelain painting skill, with elaborate designs rendered in gold paint against a black or crimson background glaze. Kutani also produces cats with realistically painted fur, such as tabby stripes.

    Temples around Japan at which Maneki Neko is

historically or legendarily important—Gotoku-ji, for instance—also feature distinctive styles of cat figurine. Gotoku-ji's Beckoning Cats are simple, pure white, adorned only with a red collar and bell. The Sumiyoshi-taisha shrine in Osaka offers kimono-clad Hattatsuneko, first mentioned in an 1876 newspaper account. Legend has it that if a person collects 48 Hattatsuneko cats, one a month over a four-year period, he or she will be ensured of good fortune.

Maneki Neko is sometimes depicted in combination with other lucky symbols. Of these, Daruma is perhaps the most familiar. A scowling, roly-poly figure clad in a red robe, Daruma is a depiction of the Bodhidharma, the founder of Zen Buddhism. A papier-mâché Daruma will usually come with blank, pupil-less eyes; the custom is to make a wish and color in one pupil. When the Daruma grants the wish, the other pupil is colored in as a thank you. Maneki Neko and Daruma together are considered especially lucky.

Other Lucky Cats appear alongside a bizarre, straw-hat-wearing figure that looks like a demented

potbellied bear. This is Tanuki, a character based on a raccoon-like native dog credited with magical shape-shifting powers. A creature of bacchanalian propensity, he is said to love sake; indeed, he is usually shown holding a flask of it in one paw, while the other clutches a promissory note with which he has "paid" for the liquor. (This subterfuge is apparently part of his charm.) In Japan, Tanuki figurines are often seen in restaurants and bars, where they beckon customers just as Lucky Cat does.

Another common variation has Maneki Neko accompanied by some or all of the Seven Lucky Gods—Ebisu, God of Good Fortune; Daikokuten, God of Wealth; Benzaiten, Goddess of the Arts; Hotei, God of Happiness; Fukorokuju, God of Wisdom; Jurojin, God of Longevity; and Bishamonten, God of Treasure and War. The gods may stand on or with the cat; some popular figurines show all eight riding a *takarabune* (treasure boat), which may be laden with bags of money and gold bars.

More unusual variations on Maneki Neko include

beckoning pigs, lucky frogs (also known as *kero kero*), lucky dogs, and lucky tigers—the last often seen dressed in a baseball cap or uniform as the team mascot for the Hanshin Tigers.

The different colors of Maneki Neko figurines also carry particular meanings. Traditionally, Beckoning Cats were white or tricolor—that is, painted with orange or red and black spots to represent calico fur. The white Maneki Neko is a symbol of purity and an all-purpose granter of good fortune. The tricolor cat also brings general luck, and its long-standing popularity may be due to a belief among sailors that a rare male calico cat is especially auspicious.

Although white and calico Maneki Neko figurines are still dominant, savvy marketing has led more recently to the development of new Maneki Neko colors, each supposedly with specialized powers. A black Maneki Neko is said to ward off evil. The power attributed to the red Maneki Neko is that of preventing illness. A yellow Beckoning Cat figurine is supposed to bring wealth, particularly, according to some sources,

when placed in the west area of one's home. Gold Maneki Nekos are also thought to be financially propitious. Blue Maneki Nekos grant luck at school and in studies, green ones bestow a green thumb, and pink ones are displayed to help their owners meet potential romantic partners and to promote successful relationships.

With a whole world of Maneki Nekos from which to choose, there is no reason not to let the magic of the Beckoning Cat into your life and heart. Ask not to whom the cat beckons, and fill your world with Maneki Neko.

How to Use Your Lucky Cat

You can enjoy your Maneki Neko figurine however you like; after all, the Lucky Cat is supposed to make you happy. If you keep him on your desk, or anywhere you often see him, he may remind you of the blessings you already enjoy. For maximum fortune-beckoning effect, however, you may choose to position your cat on its altar facing a doorway through which luck may arrive.